# THE BEST OF
# ITALY

# THE BEST OF
# ITALY
## A COOKBOOK

Evie Righter

Recipes by Georgia Downard

CollinsPublishersSanFrancisco

*A Division of HarperCollinsPublishers*

First published in USA 1992 by Collins Publishers San Francisco

Produced by Smallwood and Stewart Inc.,
New York City

© 1992 Smallwood and Stewart

Edited by Melanie Falick

Library of Congress Cataloging-in-Publication Data

Righter, Evie
    The Best of Italy/Evie Righter.
        p.   cm.
    Includes index.
    ISBN 0-00-255085-7
    1. Cookery, Italian.   I. Title.
    TX723.R526   1992
    641.5945—dc20          91-45252

Printed in China

5  7  9  10  8  6  4

# Contents

# Introduction

THE BEST OF ITALY is a collection of nearly fifty recipes representing the splendors of the Italian kitchen. But what is it exactly that is so very pleasing about Italian cooking, that makes one smile, even glow, at the prospect of cooking or dining Italian? It is more than her singular world-class pasta dishes ~ although some might argue with this ~ or her variety of veal preparations available nowhere else in the world. Is it the cheeses ~ the Parmigianos, especially the world's favorite, Parmigiano-Reggiano, as well as the fontina, gorgonzola, and mozzarella? Think of the breads, the hams and salamis and prosciuttos. What would we do without the remarkable olive oils and aged balsamic vinegar ... and the wines? It is, in part, this spectacular variety of wonderful ingredients and preparations that makes Italian cuisine so appealing.

*Olive pickers near Siracusa*

We must also remember the philosophy the Italian people share about family and food. Let us consider how the Italians themselves dine. Home cooking is important and so is the family, and at the Sunday afternoon meal, or during the week for that matter, the entire family sits down ~ generations at a time, grandparents and *bambini* alike. The pasta sauce has been cooking for hours; in many instances the pasta dough is also freshly made. There is pride in this cooking that goes way beyond the table. It is inherited; it is real and alive.

To this we must add the fact that the Italian peninsula, surrounded as it is by water on three sides, provides such diversity of terrain that each region boasts its own wealth with which these home cooks, and chefs, can improvise. In the north of Italy are wheat fields, and from these we derive so many marvelous breads. In the Po Valley are rice fields, from which we inherit *risotto*. From Tuscany, we get olive oil, beef and artichokes; from its shores, an unbelievable variety of seafood. And in the south, the tomato reigns. Call it pride of place or origin, perhaps, but Italian cooking is intensely regional, and just by looking at the ingredients of a recipe you will come to know its source.

There is the historical factor, as well. Sitting as it does at the crossroads of southern Europe, Italy has been visited by the Greeks, the Arabs, the French, the Spanish, and the Germans, all of whom have left a mark on Italian culture and on Italian cuisine.

So when I say that THE BEST OF ITALY provides a sampling of splendid Italian cooking, it is with the understanding that not even a longer collection of recipes could include all of Italy's culinary treasures. Here is a start: tempting *antipasti; primi piatti,* first courses that include soups and a *frittata,* or omelet; a handful of pasta dishes with three different pasta doughs and sauces as well, plus a red-, white-, and green-colored *lasagne.* You will recognize the names of many of the main courses: classics like *bollito misto, saltimbocca, ossobuco.* And, finally, breads and *pizza* and four very different desserts.

A word about the equipment and ingredients called for in the recipes: Medium-size saucepans are understood throughout. Unless otherwise stated, olive oil should be pure or virgin, not extra-virgin, which is reserved for those recipes (mainly the uncooked ones) in which the flavor of the very best olive oil will shine through. Eggs are large, black pepper is freshly ground, lemon juice is freshly squeezed, and butter is sweet not salted. I urge you always to keep fresh herbs on hand. It goes without saying, of course, that the better the ingredients put into a recipe the better the results.

With that I wish you *buon appetito*!

Evie Righter

# Antipasti

## Assorted Italian Appetizers

The world has come to recognize *antipasti* as the wonderful selection of foods that begin an Italian meal. This recipe celebrates much of the best of Italy ~ Parmesan, prosciutto, roasted red peppers, mozzarella ~ without being specific to any one region. Vary it as you will, but be sure to serve it with crusty Italian bread.

*2 cups marinated bocconcini*
*(small mozzarella balls)*
*2 (7-ounce) cans Italian tuna*
*packed in oil, drained & flaked*
*1½ cups Roasted Bell Peppers (p. 70)*

*1½ cups marinated mushrooms,*
*drained*
*1 cup oil-cured black olives, drained*
*4 slices Parmesan, cut ¼ inch thick*
*4 slices prosciutto*

Place the mozzarella in the middle of a large serving plate and arrange the remaining ingredients around it in a decorative pattern. Serve with crusty Italian bread. **Serves 4.**

# Bruschetta con Pomodori

## Garlic Bread with Tomatoes

For the Roman version of this appetizer, omit the tomato topping entirely: Simply grill the rounds, preferably over hot coals, and brush them with the garlic-flavored olive oil. *Bruschetta* can be served as an appetizer or as an accompaniment to the salad course.

6 slices crusty Italian bread, halved
   crosswise
1 large garlic clove, crushed &
   minced
4 tablespoons extra-virgin olive oil
6 large, firm ripe tomatoes, peeled,
   seeded, & chopped

Salt & pepper
¼ cup minced fresh basil leaves
1 tablespoon balsamic vinegar,
   or to taste

Preheat the broiler. Arrange the slices of bread on a baking sheet and broil 5 inches from the heat until lightly browned. Turn and brown the other side.

In a small bowl, combine the garlic and 3 tablespoons of the olive oil, and brush the mixture on one side of the bread slices.

In a skillet, heat the remaining 1 tablespoon of oil over medium heat, add the tomatoes and salt and pepper, and toss for 1 to 2 minutes, or until the tomatoes are just heated through. Stir in the basil and vinegar. Top the toasted slices with the tomato mixture. **Serves 6.**

# Prosciutto e Melone

## Prosciutto and Melon

Prosciutto coupled with ripe melon makes for a juxtaposition of textures, flavors, and colors that is at once arresting and sublime. For best results, look for *prosciutto di Parma* from Northern Italy, which is considered by many to be the most succulent prosciutto available. The melon, be it cantaloupe or honeydew, should be at its ripest. Fresh figs make a fine substitute for the melon.

*1 ripe, medium cantaloupe*
*or small honeydew melon, cut*
*into 6 wedges, rind removed*
*6 paper-thin slices prosciutto*

Divide the melon and prosciutto among 6 serving plates, arranging the prosciutto over the fruit decoratively. **Serves 6.**

*A hilltop in the Chianti region*

# Caponata

### E g g p l a n t   S a l a d

The bold, uninhibited flavors of *caponata* derive from
Sicily ~ island of hot days and unrelenting sun. This spread
can be served as a starter, with raw vegetables for dipping, as
a stuffing for tomatoes, or as an accompaniment to
grilled meats or fish.

*1 medium eggplant (about 1¼
pounds), trimmed & cut into
1-inch pieces*

*Salt*

*1 cup minced celery*

*1 cup minced red onion*

*Pepper*

*¼ cup olive oil*

*4 large plum tomatoes, peeled,
seeded, & chopped*

*⅓ cup red wine vinegar combined
with 1 teaspoon sugar*

*2 tablespoons drained capers*

*4 anchovy fillets, minced (optional)*

*2 teaspoons tomato paste*

*3 tablespoons minced fresh basil
leaves or 1 teaspoon dried*

*¼ cup pitted black olives, chopped*

*¼ cup minced parsley*

In a colander, sprinkle the eggplant with salt and let its bitter juices drain off for 30 minutes. Rinse the eggplant and pat dry.

In a skillet over medium heat, cook the celery and onion with salt and pepper in half the olive oil, stirring occasionally, for 10 minutes. Reserve in a bowl. Add the remaining oil to the skillet and warm it over medium heat until hot. Add all the eggplant and cook, stirring occasionally,

*Olive groves near Calabria*

for 6 to 8 minutes, or until lightly browned. Add the celery-onion mixture, the tomatoes, vinegar mixture, capers, anchovies, tomato paste, basil, and salt and pepper, and simmer, partially covered, stirring occasionally, for 15 minutes. Stir in the olives, parsley, and more salt and pepper to taste. Let the mixture cool, then cover and chill overnight. **Serves 6.**

# Insalata di Calamari e Fagioli

## Squid and Bean Salad

Italian cooks have long appreciated the delicate flavor and
unique texture of squid. In this recipe, it is coupled
with cannellini beans, another Italian favorite, and dressed
with olive oil and fresh lemon juice. In larger servings,
this salad makes a refreshing main course for
a luncheon or supper.

*1½ pounds squid, cleaned, tentacles
& flaps removed, body sacs
cut crosswise into ¼-inch-
wide rings*

*¼ pound dried cannellini beans,
cooked according to package
directions, or 1½ cups drained
canned cannellini beans*

*1 cup sliced celery*

*1 small red onion, sliced into rings*

*2 tablespoons lemon juice, or to taste*

*6 tablespoons extra-virgin olive oil,
or to taste*

*3 tablespoons minced parsley*

*Salt & pepper*

Bring a large saucepan of salted water to a boil. Add the squid and simmer gently, stirring, for 1 minute, or until no longer transparent, but just opaque. Drain and pat dry with paper towels.

In a serving bowl, combine the squid, drained beans, celery, and onion. Add the lemon juice, olive oil, parsley, and salt and pepper. Toss lightly to combine. **Serves 4.**

# Cappelletti in Brodo

### Small Stuffed Pasta in Broth

Pasta dumplings that are in the shape of little peaked hats
and are filled with either cheese or meat are called *cappelletti*
in Bologna but *tortellini* in Romagna. Whatever the name,
they are delicious either in soup, as they are traditionally
served and are used in this recipe, or in cream
or tomato sauces.

½ pound cappelletti, tortellini,
or raviolini
8 cups beef broth
Salt & pepper

3 tablespoons minced parsley
Freshly grated Parmesan as an
accompaniment

In a large saucepan of boiling salted water, cook the pasta, stirring occasionally, for 6 to 8 minutes, or until just tender. Drain and refresh under cold water. Drain again.

Just before serving, bring the broth to a boil in a saucepan and season it with salt and pepper. Add the cooked pasta and simmer until just heated through. To serve, divide the soup among four bowls and sprinkle each with some of the parsley. Serve the cheese at the table. **Serves 4.**

# Zuppa di Pesce

## Fish Soup with Assorted Shellfish

Whether it is called *cacciucco* or *brodetto*, as in Southern
Italy, or *zuppa di pesce*, as it is known in the North, it is
Italian fish soup, big and flavorful. The more
varied the seafood the better.

1 cup finely chopped fennel

1 cup finely chopped leek

1 tablespoon minced garlic

1 teaspoon dried thyme

1 teaspoon dried oregano

¼ cup minced fresh basil leaves or
    1 teaspoon dried

1 teaspoon fennel seeds, crushed

Salt & pepper

¼ cup olive oil

1 cup dry white wine

6 cups fish stock or 2 cups bottled
    clam juice with 4 cups water

1 (28-ounce) can crushed tomatoes
    in purée

½ pound squid, cleaned

1 dozen mussels, cleaned

1 dozen small cherrystone clams, cleaned

2 pounds firm-fleshed white fish,
    such as sea bass or red snapper
    fillets, cut into 2-inch pieces

½ pound large shrimp, shelled and
    deveined

Minced fresh basil leaves or
    parsley for garnish

In a casserole over medium heat, cook the fennel, leek, garlic, dried herbs, and salt and pepper in the olive oil, stirring occasionally, for 5 minutes. Add the wine, stock, tomatoes in purée, and squid. Bring the liquid to a boil and simmer, covered, stirring occasionally, for 30 minutes, or until the squid is tender. Add the mussels

*An early morning fish market in Reggio Calabria*

and clams, bring the liquid to a boil, and cook over medium heat, covered, for 5 minutes. Add the fish and shrimp and simmer the soup, covered, for 5 to 8 minutes, or until the mussel and clam shells have opened and the fish is still firm. Discard any shellfish that have not opened. Season the soup with salt and pepper and garnish with the basil or parsley. Serve the soup in large bowls. **Serves 6.**

# Minestrone

## Vegetable and Bean Soup

Though *minestrone* can be considered the national dish of
Italy, its ingredients vary from place to place. Here, it boasts
green beans, cannellini beans, and pasta; variations might
include any number of vegetables ~ potatoes, cabbage, carrots,
or zucchini, for example ~ as well as rice, chick-peas, or bacon.

1½ cups minced onion

1½ cups minced carrot

1½ cups minced celery

¼ cup olive oil

1 (28-ounce) can crushed tomatoes,
 including liquid

6 cups chicken stock or water

2 tablespoons minced fresh basil
 leaves or ½ teaspoon dried

½ teaspoon dried thyme

½ teaspoon fennel seeds, crushed

Salt & pepper

¼ pound green beans, trimmed &
 cut into 1-inch lengths

½ cup small pasta shapes, such as
 tubetti or shells

¼ pound dried cannellini beans,
 cooked according to package
 directions, or 1½ cups
 drained canned cannellini beans

2 garlic cloves, minced

⅓ cup minced fresh basil leaves
 or parsley

In a casserole over low heat, cook the
onion, carrot, and celery in the olive oil,
stirring occasionally, for 5 minutes. Add
the tomatoes with their liquid, the stock,
basil, thyme, fennel, and salt and pepper,
and bring the liquid to a boil. Cover and
simmer, stirring occasionally, for 20 minutes. Add the green beans and pasta and

simmer for 10 minutes, or until the beans and pasta are just tender. Add the drained cannellini beans, garlic, and salt and pep- per, and simmer, stirring occasionally, until the beans are heated through. Stir in the ⅓ cup fresh herbs. **Serves 6.**

# Frittata di Asparagi

## Asparagus Omelet

A *frittata* is an open-faced Italian omelet. Some *frittate*, like the one here, employ vegetables, others cooked pasta, grated cheese, or chopped prosciutto. The simplest version of all, perhaps, calls only for a sprinkling of balsamic vinegar over the top. To make a *frittata* successfully, you will need a good heavy-bottomed skillet.

½ pound pencil-thin asparagus, trimmed & cut into 1-inch lengths

6 eggs

½ cup freshly grated Parmesan

Salt & pepper

4 tablespoons butter

1 small red onion, minced

Preheat the broiler. In a saucepan of boiling salted water, blanch the asparagus for 30 seconds to 1 minute, or until just tender. Drain and refresh under cold water.

In a bowl, whisk the eggs with ⅓ cup of the Parmesan and salt and pepper. In a 12-inch nonstick skillet over medium heat, warm the butter until hot. Add the onion and cook, stirring occasionally, for 3 minutes. Add the asparagus pieces and cook, stirring, for 1 minute more. Pour the beaten eggs into the skillet, reduce the heat to low, and cook the mixture, covered, for 8 minutes, or until the eggs are almost set.

Sprinkle the top of the *frittata* with the remaining cheese. Place under the broiler about 4 inches from the heat and cook for 1 to 2 minutes, or until the eggs are set. Cut into wedges and serve. **Serves 4 to 6.**

*Cathedral of Santa Maria del Fiore, Florence*

# Pasta all'Uovo

## Fresh Pasta Dough

A food processor can combine and knead pasta dough in a fraction of the time it would take to make that same dough by hand. To roll out the dough, we suggest using a pasta machine. Start with the blade to cut *fettuccine*, as it is probably the blade you will use most often. Let the strands of pasta dry at room temperature, then wrap them in plastic bags and store in the refrigerator for up to three days. To cook fresh pasta, allow just a few minutes, and in some cases ~ with thin noodles, for example ~ not even that long.

*2¼ cups plus 1 tablespoon unbleached flour*

*½ teaspoon salt*
*4 large eggs, lightly beaten*

In a food processor, combine the 2¼ cups flour and the salt. With the motor running, add the eggs and process the dough, adding the remaining 1 tablespoon flour, until it forms a ball. Process for 20 seconds to knead the dough.

Remove the dough from the processor, cover it with an inverted bowl, and let rest at room temperature for 1 hour. Knead and roll the pasta dough as described below. **Makes about 1 pound.**

To Knead and Roll Pasta Dough

Set the rollers of a pasta machine at the largest notch and divide the dough into four pieces. Work with one piece of dough

at a time and cover the remaining pieces with an inverted bowl. Pat down the dough so that it is thin enough to fit through the largest notch on the pasta machine (about ¼ inch thick). Lightly sprinkle the dough with flour and feed it through the rollers. Fold the rolled dough in half, turn it, and feed it through the rollers 8 to 10 more times, folding it in half and turning it each time. Turn the dial down one notch and feed the dough through without folding it. Turn the dial one notch down each time until the lowest notch is reached. Roll the remaining pieces of pasta dough in the same manner and cut the dough into the desired shape.

# Pasta Verde

When spinach is added to plain pasta dough, it changes the color but not the taste or nutritional value. It can be used interchangeably with plain dough, and is especially attractive when combined with tomato sauces.

*2⅓ cups plus 1 tablespoon*
*unbleached flour*
*½ teaspoon salt*

*½ cup cooked, drained, & squeezed*
*dry spinach, chopped*
*3 large eggs, lightly beaten*

In a food processor, combine the 2⅓ cups flour, the salt, and the spinach. With the motor running, add the eggs and process the dough, adding the remaining 1 tablespoon flour, until it forms a ball. Process for 20 seconds to knead the dough.

Remove the dough from the processor, cover it with an inverted bowl, and let rest at room temperature for 1 hour. Knead and roll the dough as described on page 28. **Makes about 1¼ pounds.**

# Pasta di Semolina

## Semolina Pasta Dough

Semolina flour, milled from hard durum wheat, can be used for any of the noodles you would make with standard unbleached flour. There is no discernible difference in flavor between plain and semolina pasta. But, because of its high gluten content, semolina flour makes a durable dough that is suitable for the most robust tomato and vegetable sauces.

*2 cups plus 1 tablespoon semolina flour (available at specialty markets)*

*½ teaspoon salt*
*4 large eggs*

In a food processor, combine the 2 cups flour and the salt. With the motor running, add the eggs and process the dough, adding the remaining 1 tablespoon flour, until it forms a ball. Process for 20 seconds to knead the dough.

Remove the dough from the processor, cover it with an inverted bowl, and let rest at room temperature for 1 hour. Knead and roll the dough as described on page 28. **Makes about 1 pound.**

# Salsa Alfredo

## Alfredo Sauce

It would be nearly impossible for this white sauce not to taste superb given its ingredients – heavy cream, butter, and Parmesan. Serve on *fettuccine* with lots of crusty bread for soaking up any sauce that remains on the plate.

6 tablespoons butter

1 cup heavy cream

½ cup freshly grated
Parmesan, or to taste

Freshly grated nutmeg

Salt & pepper

Melt the butter in a saucepan over medium heat. Add the cream and cook, stirring, until it comes to a simmer. Remove the pan from the heat and add the Parmesan, a little at a time, stirring, until all of it is incorporated. Season the sauce with the nutmeg and salt and pepper. **Makes about 1½ cups.**

# Pesto

## Basil, Parmesan, and Pine Nut Sauce

There are few sauces that compare with this renowned creation from Genoa. Originally, and in some places still, *pesto* is made with a mortar and pestle; hence, the word "pesto," which derives from the verb "pestare," meaning "to pound." Use the most fragrant basil and the best olive oil and Parmesan available. Serve *pesto* over pasta or a salad, or use it as a dipping sauce or as an enhancement for vegetable soups.

2 cups fresh basil leaves

2 garlic cloves, chopped

½ cup freshly grated Parmesan,
preferably Parmigiano-Reggiano

⅔ cup extra-virgin olive oil

¼ cup pine nuts

Salt & pepper

In a food processor, combine all the ingredients and blend until thoroughly combined. **Makes about 1½ cups.**

# Salsa Marinara

## Marinara Sauce

There are many tomato sauces in Italian cooking. Some use butter as a base, others olive oil with or without chopped vegetables. This one combines olive oil with just onion, garlic, and tomatoes. Its flavor is pure and clean, and it can be used on any number of pastas or combined with meatballs as suggested on page 60. If you cannot find very ripe fresh tomatoes, use two (28-ounce) cans peeled, whole San Marzano tomatoes.

*1 onion, minced*

*2 garlic cloves, minced*

*½ cup olive oil*

*2 pounds ripe tomatoes, cored &*
*cut into 1-inch pieces*

*Pinch of sugar*

*Salt & pepper*

In a medium-large saucepan over medium heat, cook the onion and garlic in the oil, stirring occasionally, for 5 minutes. Stir in the tomatoes, sugar, and salt and pepper, and simmer, covered, stirring occasionally, for 25 minutes. Purée the mixture through the fine disc of a food mill into a saucepan. Simmer the purée, stirring occasionally, for 15 minutes. **Makes about 3 cups.**

# Fettuccine al Pesto

**Fettuccine with Pesto**

Not every sauce is suited to every pasta. You wouldn't,
for example, weigh down delicate *spaghettini* with a heavy
meat topping. In this recipe, the *fettuccine* catches and holds
onto the creamy herb sauce. Other pasta shapes that will
work well are *linguine* and *fusilli*.

*1 pound fettuccine*

*1 recipe Pesto Sauce (p. 34)*

*Fresh basil leaves for garnish*

Bring a large saucepan of salted water to a boil. Add the *fettuccine* and cook, stirring occasionally, until *al dente*. Drain the pasta, transfer it to a heated serving bowl, and toss it with the *pesto*. Garnish with the fresh basil leaves and serve at once. **Serves 4 to 6.**

# Pasta con Melanzane e Pomodori

### Spaghetti with Roasted Eggplant and Tomatoes

In the extensive repertoire of Italian sauces, there are many
that combine eggplant and tomatoes. This one is particularly
appealing because the eggplant is roasted rather than fried,
the more usual preparation. What you end up with is no less
delicious, but it is lighter. You could also use this sauce
as a topping for plain *bruschetta*.

*1-1¼ pounds eggplant, trimmed &
 halved lengthwise*

*⅓ cup olive oil*

*1 onion, minced*

*2 large garlic cloves, minced*

*1 (28-ounce) can crushed tomatoes
 in purée*

*Salt & pepper*

*2 tablespoons minced fresh basil leaves*

*1 pound spaghetti*

Preheat the oven to 400°F. Arrange the eggplant, cut-side down, on an oiled baking sheet and bake until tender, about 20 to 25 minutes. Let cool, remove the skin, and coarsely chop the pulp.

In a skillet over medium heat, warm the oil until hot. Add the onion and garlic and cook, stirring, for 3 minutes. Add the tomatoes and simmer, stirring occasionally, for 10 to 12 minutes, or until thick. Add the chopped eggplant and salt and pepper, and simmer, stirring occasionally,

for 5 minutes, or until heated through. Stir in the basil. Keep the sauce warm.

Bring a large saucepan of salted water to a boil. Add the *spaghetti* and cook until *al dente*. Drain, transfer to a heated bowl, and toss gently with the sauce. **Serves 4 to 6.**

# Lasagne con Spinaci e Funghi

## Spinach and Mushroom Lasagne

Even though a *lasagne* recipe may look daunting in length, its various components ~ the pasta, filling, and sauces ~ if taken one-by-one, are easy to make. Furthermore, it can be made a day in advance and kept in the refrigerator overnight. A wonderful dish for company, this vegetarian *lasagne* is especially attractive when sliced, studded as it is with the colors of the Italian flag.

*2 pounds spinach, trimmed & washed*

*2 onions, minced*

*4 tablespoons olive oil*

*1 pound mushrooms, sliced*

*1 teaspoon dried oregano*

*¼ cup minced fresh basil leaves*

*Salt & pepper*

*2 large garlic cloves, minced*

*⅓ cup minced fresh basil leaves or parsley*

*1 recipe Marinara Sauce (p. 35)*

*1 recipe White Sauce (p. 43)*

*½ pound lasagne noodles*

*1 pound mozzarella, grated*

*1½ cups freshly grated Parmesan*

*Fresh parsley for garnish*

In a large covered saucepan over medium heat, cook the spinach in just the water remaining on its leaves, stirring occasionally, until wilted. Drain, refresh under cold water, and squeeze dry. Coarsely chop the spinach.

In a skillet over medium heat, cook the onions in 3 tablespoons of the oil, stirring occasionally, for 5 to 7 minutes, or until golden. Add the mushrooms, oregano, basil, and salt and pepper, and cook, stirring occasionally, for 5 to 7 minutes, or until the mushrooms are firm and the liquid has evaporated. Add the spinach and garlic and cook, stirring, for 3 minutes. Set aside.

Make both the marinara and white sauces. To make the vegetable filling, in a bowl, combine the spinach mixture and the white sauce with the fresh basil or parsley.

Cook the *lasagne* noodles in rapidly boiling water for 8 to 10 minutes, until *al dente*, or according to the directions on the package. Drain and transfer to a bowl of cold water to which the remaining tablespoon of olive oil has been added (to prevent the noodles from sticking together).

Preheat the oven to 400°F. To assemble the *lasagne*, coat the bottom of an oiled 13-by 10-by 2-inch shallow baking dish with 1 cup of the marinara sauce. Cover with one-third of the pasta, arranging it in a layer over the sauce. Smooth one-third of the vegetable filling over the pasta and sprinkle with one-third of the mozzarella and Parmesan. Layer half the remaining pasta over the cheese, and top with half the remaining vegetable filling and cheese. Arrange the final layer of pasta and filling and spoon the remaining marinara sauce over the filling. Sprinkle with the remaining cheese. Bake for 30 to 35 minutes, or until bubbling. Let the *lasagne* rest for at least 10 minutes before serving. Cut it into squares, garnish with fresh parsley and serve. **Serves 6.**

# Salsa Balsamella

## White Sauce

When making this basic white sauce, be careful to whisk the mixture constantly while adding the milk and whisk again as it cooks. If not, the flour will remain unincorporated, and the sauce will be lumpy. *Salsa balsamella*, which is intrinsic to the *lasagne* recipe on page 41, can be embellished with cheese and used as a topping for baked vegetables such as cauliflower, broccoli, or small white onions.

*2½ cups milk*

*4 tablespoons butter*

*¼ cup flour*

*Salt & pepper*

*Freshly grated nutmeg*

In a saucepan, scald the milk. Cover the pan and keep the milk hot.

In another saucepan, melt the butter over medium-low heat. Add the flour and whisk the mixture for 3 minutes. Add the hot milk in a stream, whisking, and simmer the sauce, whisking occasionally, for 5 minutes. Add the salt, pepper, and nutmeg to taste. (If not using the sauce immediately, place a buttered round of wax paper directly on the surface to prevent a skin from forming.) **Makes about 2 cups.**

# Polenta con Funghi

## Cornmeal with Mushrooms

Long ago the Italians discovered that cornmeal had many culinary possibilities, and it became a regular part of their diet, particularly in the Veneto region in the north. Very accommodating and delicious, *polenta* (a sort of cornmeal porridge) can be seasoned simply with butter and cheese; it can be layered with cheese, wild mushrooms, and *balsamella*; it can accompany rich stews; or it can be fried, as below. For best results in this recipe, use coarsely ground cornmeal.

*3 ½ cups water*

*1 teaspoon salt*

*1 cup cornmeal*

*4 tablespoons butter*

*Salt & pepper*

*6 tablespoons olive oil*

*1 pound mushrooms, sliced*

*1 large clove garlic, minced*

*2 teaspoons minced fresh thyme*

*or ½ teaspoon dried*

*Salt & pepper*

*Fresh thyme sprigs for garnish*

In a saucepan over high heat, bring the water and salt to a boil. Reduce the heat to medium and add the cornmeal in a stream, whisking constantly. Cook over medium-low heat, stirring frequently, for 15 minutes, or until the mixture is thick. Stir in the butter and season with pepper, then pour the *polenta* into a buttered 9-inch-square shallow baking pan to cool. Cover and chill for at least 30 minutes.

Invert the chilled *polenta* onto a board and cut it into eight squares. In a large

nonstick skillet over medium-high heat, warm 3 tablespoons of the oil until hot. Add the *polenta* squares and cook for 2 to 3 minutes on each side, without browning them, until heated through. Transfer to a platter and keep warm.

In a large skillet over medium-high heat, warm the remaining oil until hot. Reduce the heat to medium and add the mushrooms, garlic, thyme, and salt and pepper. Cook the mixture, stirring occasionally, for 5 to 7 minutes, or until the mushrooms are firm and the liquid has evaporated. Spoon over the *polenta* and garnish with the fresh thyme sprigs. **Serves 4.**

# Gnocchi alla Marinara

## Potato Dumplings with Marinara Sauce

In Italy, *gnocchi*, Italian dumplings, are served as a first course and precede, depending upon their sauce, braised or roasted meat or poultry. *Gnocchi* can be made with a potato dough, as they are here, or with semolina dough or a ricotta-and-spinach mixture. No matter what the ingredients, the one characteristic they should all have in common is their lightness. *Gnocchi* lend themselves to a variety of sauces, including marinara and *pesto*. They are also appetizing simply mixed with melted butter and fresh sage.

1 pound Idaho potatoes

Salt

1 egg yolk

Freshly grated nutmeg

White pepper

1 cup unbleached flour

1 recipe Marinara Sauce (p. 35)

In a saucepan, combine the potatoes with enough water to cover them by 2 inches. Add salt to taste. Cover the pan and bring the water to a boil. Reduce the heat and simmer for 25 to 30 minutes, or until tender. Drain the potatoes, then return them to the pan and shake them over medium heat to dry them, about 2 to 3 minutes. Let the potatoes cool slightly, then peel them and force them through a potato ricer into a bowl. Alternatively, mash them with a potato masher. Beat in the egg yolk, nutmeg, salt, and white pepper. Stir in the flour, a little at a time, until completely incorporated.

To shape *gnocchi*, divide the dough into

about six pieces. Flour your hands and a work surface. (Keep your hands and the work surface floured throughout the rolling and cutting process.) Shape each piece of dough into a roll about 1 inch in diameter. Cut the rolls into ¾-inch lengths and, with your index finger, press each piece against the tines of a fork to form a decorative design.

To cook, bring a large saucepan of salted water to a boil. Add the *gnocchi* and adjust the heat to keep the water at a slow boil. Cook the *gnocchi*, stirring gently, until they begin to rise to the surface, about 2 to 3 minutes. With a skimmer, transfer the *gnocchi* to a serving dish and spoon the marinara sauce over them. **Serves 4 to 6.**

*The Galleria, Milan*

# Risotto alla Milanese

## Milan-style Rice

*Risotto*, the singularly wonderful cooked rice of Italy, is unfailingly served as a first course, except when it is prepared *alla Milanese*, in which case it accompanies *Ossobuco* (p. 64) as a second course. *Risotto* should only be made with short-grain Italian Arborio rice, which has the ability to absorb a lot of liquid without becoming mushy. The keys to success when preparing this dish are stirring the rice continuously and serving it immediately once it is ready.

1 cup minced onion

6 tablespoons softened butter

2 cups Arborio rice

½ cup dry white wine

5 to 6 cups homemade chicken stock or canned broth, heated

½ teaspoon saffron threads, crumbled

⅓ cup freshly grated Parmesan

In a heavy saucepan over medium heat, cook the onion in 3 tablespoons of the butter, stirring occasionally, for 3 minutes. Add the rice and stir to coat it with the butter. Add the wine and simmer, stirring, until it is reduced by half. Add ½ cup of the heated stock or broth and simmer the rice, stirring, until almost all of the liquid is absorbed. Stirring constantly, add about 5 cups of the stock, ½ cup at a time, waiting until the rice has absorbed all of the liquid before adding the next ½ cup. This will take a total of about 25 minutes. The risotto should be creamy but still *al dente*.

In a small bowl, combine the saffron with ¼ cup of the remaining stock and stir the mixture into the hot rice. Add the remaining 3 tablespoons butter and the Parmesan, and stir gently to combine. Serve at once. **Serves 6.**

# Gamberi con Aglio al Burro

## Shrimp in Garlic Butter

Intuitively, Italian cooks seem to understand how to use a
minimal number of ingredients to showcase the wealth of
seafood caught in their waters. Here, shrimp are grilled, still
in the shell, then doused with garlic butter. Serve with plenty
of bread to soak up the butter.

6 tablespoons butter, melted

6 tablespoons olive oil

2 tablespoons lemon juice

3 garlic cloves, crushed & minced

¼ cup minced parsley

Salt & pepper

24 jumbo shrimp, split lengthwise,
leaving feet on & shells intact,
cleaned & patted dry

In a small bowl, combine the butter, olive oil, lemon juice, garlic, 2 tablespoons of the parsley, and salt and pepper.

Preheat the broiler.

One at a time, dip the shrimp into the butter-garlic sauce and arrange them, shell-side down, in one layer in a baking dish. Broil the shrimp about 5 inches from the heat for 10 to 12 minutes, or until firm. Arrange the shrimp on a serving dish, pour the sauce in the pan over them, and sprinkle the remaining parsley on top. **Serves 6.**

*Traditional fishing, Pescara*

# Pesce all'Olio di Oliva ed Erbe Fresche

## Roasted Fish with Olive Oil and Fresh Herbs

In this simple recipe, a small number of ingredients is used so as to complement the flavor of the fish rather than overwhelm it. The olive oil-lemon juice marinade keeps the fish moist as it bakes.

1 (2½-3 pound) whole fish, such as red snapper or striped bass, cleaned but with head & tail

⅓ cup olive oil

2 tablespoons lemon juice

2 garlic cloves, finely minced

1½ teaspoons minced fresh rosemary or ½ teaspoon dried

1½ teaspoons minced fresh thyme or ½ teaspoon dried

Salt & pepper

Lemon slices and fresh herbs for garnish

Arrange the fish in an oiled shallow baking pan. In a small bowl, combine the olive oil, lemon juice, garlic, rosemary, thyme, and salt and pepper, and pour the mixture over the fish, coating the insides as well. Chill the fish, covered loosely with plastic wrap, for 2 to 4 hours.

Preheat the oven to 450°F.

Bake the fish for 20 to 25 minutes, or until it flakes easily when tested with a fork. (Cooking time will vary depending upon the size of the fish.) Garnish with the lemon slices and fresh herbs. **Serves 4.**

# Passera di Mare alla Salsa di Pomodoro Piccante

## Baked Fish with Spicy Tomato Sauce

For this recipe, it is important to choose firm-fleshed fish steaks, ones that will hold up to browning and baking and to the robust flavor of this tomato-based sauce. If desired, make the sauce hotter by increasing the red pepper to ½ teaspoon.

2 pounds fish steaks, such as halibut or swordfish, cut 1 inch thick

Flour for dredging

Salt & pepper

7 tablespoons olive oil

1 onion, minced

1 stalk celery, sliced

2 garlic cloves, minced

1 cup dry white wine

2 cups drained, chopped tomatoes or 1 (28-ounce) can peeled tomatoes, drained & chopped

½ teaspoon dried thyme

½ teaspoon fennel seeds, crushed

¼ teaspoon crushed red pepper, or to taste

1 (¾-1 pound) eggplant, trimmed & cut into ¼-inch slices

½ cup pitted green olives

Dredge the fish with the flour, shaking off the excess, and season with salt and pepper. In a large skillet over medium-high heat, warm 3 tablespoons of the oil until hot. Add the fish and cook for 2 minutes on each side, or until golden. Transfer to a plate.

Add 2 tablespoons of the oil to the skillet. Over medium-high heat, warm the oil until hot, then add the onion, celery, and garlic, and cook, stirring occasionally, for

5 minutes. Add the wine and reduce it by half. Add the tomatoes, thyme, fennel, red pepper, and salt and pepper. Cover and simmer for 15 minutes.

Preheat the broiler. Sprinkle the eggplant with salt and let it drain in a colander for 15 minutes. Pat dry. Brush with the remaining 2 tablespoons olive oil and season with pepper. Broil the eggplant about 4 inches from the heat for 6 minutes, or until golden on each side. Let cool.

Preheat the oven to 450°F. Arrange the fish in one layer in a shallow baking pan and layer the eggplant around the fish. Add the olives to the sauce, then spoon the sauce over the fish and eggplant. Bake for 10 to 15 minutes, or until the fish flakes easily. Transfer the fish and eggplant to a serving plate and keep warm. On the stovetop over high heat, reduce the cooking liquid, stirring, until it is thick. Spoon the sauce over the fish. **Serves 4 to 6.**

# Pollo alla Cacciatora

## Chicken with Tomatoes and Bell Peppers

Meat, game, or poultry can be cooked *alla cacciatora*, or "in the hunter's style," though the style seems to vary from cook to cook. Generally, these dishes include onions and other vegetables. In this version, the tomatoes, wine, and herbs add a great deal of the flavor. In some recipes, olives and/or anchovies are included.

*1 (3-pound) chicken, cut into serving pieces, rinsed, & patted dry*

*Salt & pepper*

*3 tablespoons olive oil*

*1 onion, sliced*

*1 large red bell pepper, cored, seeded, & cut into strips*

*2 garlic cloves, minced*

*½ cup dry white wine*

*2 cups drained, peeled, & chopped tomatoes or 1 (28-ounce) can peeled tomatoes, drained & chopped*

*1 teaspoon minced fresh oregano or ½ teaspoon dried*

*1 teaspoon minced fresh thyme or ½ teaspoon dried*

*1 bay leaf*

*2 tablespoons minced fresh basil leaves*

Season the chicken with salt and pepper. In a large skillet over medium heat, cook the chicken in 2 tablespoons of the oil, turning occasionally, for 5 to 7 minutes, or until browned. Transfer the chicken to a plate. Add the remaining 1 tablespoon of oil to the skillet and heat it until hot. Add the onion, bell pepper, and garlic, and cook, stirring occasionally, for 5 minutes. Add the wine and reduce for 1 minute.

Add the tomatoes, oregano, thyme, bay leaf, and salt and pepper, and bring the mixture to a simmer.

Return the chicken to the skillet and simmer, covered, for 25 to 30 minutes, or until the juices run clear. Transfer the chicken to a serving platter. Reduce the vegetable mixture in the skillet, stirring, until it is thick, about 3 minutes. Spoon the vegetable mixture over the chicken. Sprinkle the dish with the basil. **Serves 4 to 6.**

# Pollo Arrosto all'Aglio e Rosmarino

## Roasted Chicken with Garlic and Rosemary

**This most simple of chicken recipes relies upon only two ingredients for flavor ~ garlic and rosemary. Both happen to be staples in the Italian kitchen. Precede this dish with *risotto* or a meat-sauced pasta.**

*1 (3½-pound) chicken, cleaned &
patted dry
2 garlic cloves, unpeeled & crushed
1 sprig fresh rosemary or
1 teaspoon dried*

*Salt & pepper
1 tablespoon butter, softened
1 tablespoon olive oil
Fresh rosemary sprigs for garnish*

Preheat the oven to 450°F.

Put the garlic and rosemary in the cavity of the chicken, and sprinkle it with salt and pepper. Truss the chicken. Rub the skin of the chicken with the butter and olive oil, and season it with salt and pepper. Roast the chicken on the rack of a roasting pan, brushing it with the pan juices, for 20 to 25 minutes, or until gold-en brown. Lower the oven temperature to 375°F. and roast the chicken, basting it frequently with the pan juices, for 30 to 35 minutes more, or until the juices run clear. Let the chicken rest, loosely covered with foil, for 10 minutes. Remove the trussing strings. Garnish with the rosemary sprigs. Serve the chicken with the pan juices. **Serves 4 to 6.**

# Polpettine alla Marinara
## Meatballs in Marinara Sauce

The success of really well-made meatballs depends upon gentle handling of the meat mixture. In this recipe, the meatballs are browned in oil as they are in Southern and Central Italy. In the North, butter is used.

⅔ cup fresh bread crumbs

¼ cup milk

½ cup minced onion

¼ cup olive oil

1 pound lean ground beef

1 egg, lightly beaten

4 tablespoons grated Parmesan

2 tablespoons minced fresh parsley

1 garlic clove, finely minced

Salt & pepper

2 cups Marinara Sauce (p. 35)

In a small bowl, soak the bread crumbs in the milk. In a skillet over medium heat, cook the onion in 2 tablespoons of the oil, stirring, for 3 minutes. In a large bowl, combine the onion mixture with the softened bread crumbs and milk, the beef, egg, Parmesan, parsley, garlic, and salt and pepper. Form the mixture into meatballs about 1½ inches in diameter.

In a large skillet over medium heat, warm the remaining 2 tablespoons of oil until hot. Add the meatballs and cook them, turning occasionally, until browned on all sides, about 10 minutes in all. Add the marinara sauce to the skillet and bring it to a simmer, stirring. Simmer for 5 minutes. If desired, serve over 1 pound of pasta. **Serves 4 to 6.**

# Saltimbocca

## Veal with Prosciutto

We have Roman culinary smarts to thank for the wonderful combination of veal, prosciutto, sage, and wine, which characterizes this dish. *Saltimbocca* is meant to be good enough to "jump into the mouth," as its name implies.

1 pound veal scaloppine, pounded ¼ inch thick and cut into 5-inch squares

2 to 3 tablespoons minced fresh sage leaves or 2½ teaspoons dried, crumbled

Salt & pepper

¼ pound thinly sliced prosciutto

2 tablespoons butter

2 tablespoons olive oil

⅔ cup dry white wine

Season both sides of the veal scaloppine with sage and salt and pepper. Top each piece of veal with a slice of prosciutto and secure the veal and prosciutto together with a toothpick.

In a skillet over medium-high heat, warm the butter and oil until hot. Add the veal bundles and cook them in batches until golden brown, about 1 minute. Reduce the heat to medium, turn the veal, and cook it for 2 minutes more.

Arrange the veal on a serving platter and remove the toothpicks. Pour off the fat in the skillet. Add the wine to the skillet and reduce it by half over medium-high heat, scraping up the brown bits that cling to the pan. Pour the sauce over the veal. **Serves 4.**

*Venice, looking toward St. Mark's*

# Ossobuco

## Braised Veal Shanks

The veal dishes of Italy are widely celebrated and among them is this preparation from Milan. Classically, the shanks are braised until fork-tender, sprinkled with *gremolata*, a mixture of lemon rind, parsley, and garlic, and then served with *Risotto alla Milanese* (p. 49).

4 pounds veal shanks

Flour for dredging

Salt & pepper

3 tablespoons butter

3 tablespoons olive oil

1 medium-large onion, minced

½ cup minced celery

½ cup minced carrot

2 large garlic cloves, minced

1 cup dry white wine

1½ cups beef stock

1½ cups canned crushed tomatoes in purée

¼ cup minced fresh basil leaves or 1 teaspoon dried

1 teaspoon dried rosemary

THE GREMOLATA:

2 tablespoons grated lemon rind

¼ cup minced parsley

1 garlic clove, finely minced

Preheat the oven to 350°F.

Dredge the veal in the flour, shaking off the excess, and sprinkle the meat with salt and pepper. In a casserole over medium heat, brown the veal in half of the butter and oil. Remove to a platter. Discard the fat from the casserole, add the remaining butter and oil, and cook the onion, celery, carrot, and garlic, still over medium heat, stirring occasionally, for 5 minutes. Add the wine and reduce it for 1 minute. Add the stock, tomatoes, herbs, and salt and pepper. Return the veal to the

casserole, bring the liquid to a simmer, and braise the veal, covered, for 1½ to 2 hours, or until tender.

Prepare the *gremolata:* In a small bowl, combine the lemon, parsley, and garlic.

When ready, remove the veal to a serving dish. Skim the fat from the cooking liquid and reduce the sauce over high heat, until slightly thickened.

Spoon the reduced sauce over the veal and sprinkle the *gremolata* over the top. **Serves 4 to 6.**

# Bollito Misto

## Assorted Boiled Meats in Broth

This is truly one of the great dishes of Northern Italy and while the ingredient list may look long, this is marvelous company food, deserving of discerning, hungry guests. Traditionally, *cotechino* (a fresh pork sausage flavored with nutmeg and cloves) and tongue are also part of the recipe but have been omitted here because real *cotechino* can be difficult to find.

*5 cups homemade beef stock or canned broth*

*1 large onion, studded with 4 cloves*

*1 large celery stalk, thickly sliced*

*1 carrot, thickly sliced*

*1 cheesecloth bag holding 1 teaspoon each dried rosemary & thyme, 8 peppercorns, 12 parsley stems, & 1 bay leaf*

*Salt & pepper*

*1 (2-pound) brisket of beef*

*1 cup peeled, seeded & chopped tomato*

*1 (2-pound) boneless brisket of veal rump, tied*

*1 (3-pound) chicken, trussed*

THE GREEN SAUCE:

*3 tablespoons minced parsley*

*2 tablespoons minced drained capers*

*4 anchovy fillets, finely minced*

*1 teaspoon minced garlic*

*1 teaspoon Dijon-style mustard*

*1 teaspoon red wine vinegar*

*⅔ cup extra-virgin olive oil*

In a large casserole or kettle, combine the beef stock, onion, celery, carrot, cheesecloth bag, and salt, and bring the liquid to a boil. Add the brisket of beef and tomato. Simmer the mixture, covered, skimming occasionally, for 1½ hours. Add the veal

rump and simmer the mixture for 45 minutes longer.

Add the chicken to the casserole and simmer, covered, for 50 minutes to 1 hour, or until the juices run clear when the chicken is pricked and both the beef and veal are tender to the touch.

Meanwhile, prepare the green sauce: In a bowl, combine the parsley, capers, anchovies, garlic, mustard, and vinegar. Add the olive oil in a stream, whisking, and whisk the sauce until well combined.

Add salt to taste. Set aside.

When the meats have finished cooking, transfer them to a large cutting board. Cut the chicken into serving pieces and the meat into slices. Strain the broth and skim its surface to remove any fat. Arrange the meats on a large heated platter and spoon the broth over all of them. Alternatively, the broth may be served separately in soup bowls as an accompaniment or as a first course. Serve with the green sauce. **Serves 6 to 8.**

# Carciofi sott'Olio

## Sautéed Artichokes

Artichokes are prepared in numerous ways in Italian cooking. They are fried whole and in pieces; they are braised; they are stuffed; they figure in stews and *risotti*. Here is a straightforward preparation, redolent of garlic and olive oil.

*Juice of ½ lemon*

*2 medium artichokes (6 to 7 ounces each), stalks trimmed to ½ inch*

*¼ cup olive oil*

*1 garlic clove, sliced*

*Salt & pepper*

In a saucepan, combine about 6 cups salted water and the lemon juice and bring to a boil. Add the trimmed artichokes and simmer, covered with wax paper and the lid, for 10 minutes. Drain the artichokes, halve them lengthwise, and remove the chokes. Pat dry.

In a medium skillet over medium-high heat, warm the oil until hot. Reduce the heat to medium, add the garlic and cook, stirring, until golden. Remove the garlic from the skillet with a slotted spoon and discard. Add the artichoke halves, cut-side down, season with salt and pepper, and cook, turning them from time to time, for 6 to 8 minutes more, or until tender. **Serves 4.**

# Peperoni Arrostiti

## Roasted Bell Peppers

Roasted bell peppers have a uniquely smoky flavor
and an appealing texture, and are superb in salads and on
*pizza*. They have also come to be expected on *antipasto*
tables throughout Italy.

*2 each green, red, & yellow bell
peppers*
*2 garlic cloves, finely minced
(optional)*
*Salt & pepper*

*2 tablespoons lemon juice*
*1 tablespoon balsamic vinegar*
*⅓ cup extra-virgin olive oil,
or to taste*

Preheat the broiler.

Arrange the bell peppers on a broiler pan and broil them about 5 inches from the heat, turning them, until charred ~ actually blackened ~ on all sides, for 15 to 20 minutes. Transfer the peppers to a paper bag or wrap them in aluminum foil and let cool. When cool enough to handle, unwrap the peppers and remove the stems. Peel the peppers, halve them, and remove the ribs.

Cut the peppers lengthwise into strips.

Arrange the peppers on a serving platter and sprinkle them with the garlic, if desired, and salt and pepper. Drizzle the lemon juice, vinegar, and oil over the peppers and let them stand, loosely covered, for 30 minutes. The peppers can be covered with plastic wrap and chilled, but should be brought back to room temperature before serving. **Serves 6.**

# Vegetali alla Griglia, con Erbe ed Aglio

## Roasted Herbed Vegetables

Herbs, garlic, and olive oil accent the vegetables in this recipe. When possible, grill them outdoors over hot coals.

*1 pound red-skinned potatoes, cut into slices*

*1 red bell pepper, cored, seeded, & quartered lengthwise*

*1 green bell pepper, cored, seeded, & quartered lengthwise*

*1 large zucchini, trimmed, halved crosswise, & each half quartered*

*2 onions, quartered*

*⅓-½ cup olive oil, or to taste*

*1½ teaspoons each fresh thyme, rosemary, & oregano or ½ teaspoon each dried*

*2 large garlic cloves, minced*

*Salt & pepper*

Preheat the oven to 400°F.

In a large, shallow oiled baking pan, combine all the ingredients and season with salt and pepper. Bake the vegetables in one layer, turning them frequently, for 30 to 45 minutes, or until tender. **Serves 6.**

*A hilltop town in Liguria*

# Insalata con Lattuga e Parmigiano

## Green Salad with Parmesan Shavings

**Above all else, an Italian green salad should be simple, its flavors pure and straightforward: excellent, fruity extra-virgin olive oil, wine vinegar, perhaps but not always a dash of balsamic vinegar, and lovely fresh greens. The Parmesan shavings in this recipe are a bonus.**

*8 cups bite-size pieces of assorted greens, such as arugula, escarole, watercress, & leaf lettuces, rinsed & patted dry*
*¼ cup minced fresh basil leaves or parsley*
*2 tablespoons white wine vinegar*

*Salt & pepper*
*⅓ cup extra-virgin olive oil*
*4 ounces Parmesan cheese, preferably Parmigiano-Reggiano, shaved into curls with a vegetable peeler*

In a salad bowl, combine the salad greens with the basil or parsley.

In a small bowl, whisk together the vinegar with salt and pepper. Add the olive oil in a stream, whisking, and whisk the dressing until emulsified. Toss the salad with the dressing. Divide the salad among six salad plates and arrange shavings of Parmesan on each serving. **Serves 6.**

# Insalata con Pomodori e Mozzarella

## Tomato and Mozzarella Salad

While the main ingredients of this combination may seem
simple, much of this salad's success depends upon your choice
of lush, vine-ripened tomatoes, fresh mozzarella, and the most
aromatic basil leaves you can find.

*2 large, vine-ripened tomatoes,*
*   cored & sliced*
*1 pound fresh mozzarella, sliced*
*1 small red onion, thinly sliced*
*   (optional)*

*Extra-virgin olive oil*
*Salt & pepper*
*Fresh basil leaves, cut into strips,*
*   to taste*

On a serving platter, arrange the tomato, mozzarella, and onion slices, overlapping them in a decorative pattern. Drizzle with the olive oil and season with salt and pepper. Sprinkle the salad with the basil. Serve at room temperature. **Serves 4 to 6.**

# Pane all'Olio

## Olive Oil Bread

The breads of Italy are deservedly famous, as satisfyingly distinct and varied as the cuisine. Some are round and chewy in texture, like the one below; others are more refined, made tender with semolina flour; and still others are studded with olives or tomatoes and burst with character and taste.

*1 package (2½ teaspoons) active dry yeast*

*¼ teaspoon sugar*

*1 cup warm water (108°-110°F.)*

*3 cups unbleached flour*

*1 tablespoon olive oil*

*1 teaspoon salt*

To make the sponge: In a bowl, proof the yeast with the sugar in ½ cup of the water for 5 minutes, or until foamy. Add 1 cup of the flour and stir to combine well. Cover with plastic wrap and let rise in a warm place for 1 to 1½ hours, or until doubled in bulk.

To make the dough: In a bowl, combine the remaining flour and water with the olive oil and salt, and form the mixture into a ball. Add the sponge to the bowl and combine both mixtures well, kneading the dough on a lightly floured surface for 8 to 10 minutes, or until smooth and elastic. Form the dough into a round loaf, place on an oiled baking sheet, and sprinkle with flour. Cover the loaf loosely and let it rise in a warm place for 1½ hours, or until doubled in bulk. While the dough is rising, preheat the oven to 400°F.

With a sharp knife or razor, make several slashes in the top of the risen loaf. Bake the loaf for 45 to 50 minutes, or until it sounds hollow when tapped on the bottom. Let the loaf cool on a rack. **Makes 1 loaf.**

# Pasta per Pizza

## Pizza Dough

The Neapolitans take credit for inventing *pizza*, but food historians agree that this most soul-satisfying of foods can be traced back to the Greeks and Romans. It was the street sellers in Naples in the nineteenth century, though, who pushed *pizza* to popularity, selling them with various toppings as snacks and even for breakfast. The mark of a really good *pizza* begins with its crust. It should be chewy, but not tough, well-wrought, but not overworked. The dough is a yeast one, but easier to make than you might think. The more you make it, the better you'll get.

*1 package (2½ teaspoons) active dry yeast*

*Pinch of sugar*

*¼ cup warm water (108°-110°F.)*

*2-2¼ cups flour*

*1 teaspoon salt*

*3 tablespoons olive oil*

In a small bowl, proof the yeast with the sugar in ½ cup of the warm water for 5 minutes, or until foamy.

In a food processor, combine 2 cups of the flour and the salt. With the motor running, pour the proofed yeast mixture, the olive oil, and the remaining ¼ cup warm water down the feed tube and process the mixture until it forms a ball, adding more flour, a little at a time, if the dough is too wet. Process for 20 seconds to knead the dough. Place the dough in an oiled bowl and turn it to coat with the oil. Let the dough rise in a warm place, covered with plastic wrap and a dish towel, for 1 to 1½ hours, or until doubled in bulk. **Makes enough dough for one 14-inch pizza.**

# Pizza Margherita

## Pizza with Tomatoes, Mozzarella, and Basil

This popular *pizza* is testimony to the enduring appeal
of fresh tomato sauce, mozzarella, and tender basil. The
anchovies in this recipe are not part of the classic
combination but have been added for extra flavor.
If desired, they may be omitted.

*1 recipe Pizza Dough (p. 77)*

*1⅔ cups grated mozzarella cheese*

*⅔-1 cup Marinara Sauce*

*(p. 35), or to taste*

*3 garlic cloves, finely minced*

*6 anchovy fillets, drained (optional)*

*2 tablespoons freshly grated*

*Parmesan*

*1 tablespoon extra-virgin olive oil*

Preheat the oven to 450°F.

On a floured surface, roll out the *pizza* dough into a ¼-inch-thick round. Fit the dough into an oiled *pizza* pan or arrange it on an oiled heavy baking sheet. Sprinkle the dough with the mozzarella and spoon the marinara sauce over it, leaving a 1-inch border. Top with the garlic and anchovies, then sprinkle on the Parmesan. Drizzle with the olive oil.

Bake the *pizza* in the lower third of the oven for 15 to 20 minutes, or until the cheese is melted and the crust is golden brown. **Serves 4 to 6.**

# Pizza con Salvio, Prosciutto, e Funghi

## Pizza with Sage, Prosciutto, and Mushrooms

Sage, prosciutto, and mushrooms ~ three important and
much-used ingredients in the Italian kitchen ~ are combined
with fontina, a mild cheese from the Valle d'Aosta region in
the northwest ~ in a *pizza* topping that is at once salty and
fragrant, savory and refined. Do try to use wild mushrooms if
you can find them: fresh *porcini* are a good choice.

*1 recipe Pizza Dough (p. 77)*

*1 red onion, minced*

*5 tablespoons extra-virgin olive oil*

*¼ pound mushrooms, trimmed &
   sliced*

*Salt & pepper*

*2 large garlic cloves, minced*

*1 tablespoon minced fresh sage or
   1 teaspoon dried, crumbled*

*1⅔ cups grated fontina or
   mozzarella cheese*

*2 ounces prosciutto, thinly sliced
   (about 3 slices)*

*2 tablespoons freshly grated
   Parmesan*

*Fresh sage leaves for garnish*

On a floured surface, roll out the *pizza* dough into a ¼-inch-thick round. Fit the dough into an oiled *pizza* pan or arrange it on an oiled heavy baking sheet.

In a skillet over medium heat, cook the onion in 3 tablespoons of the oil, stirring occasionally, for 5 to 7 minutes, or until golden. Add the mushrooms and salt and pepper, and cook, stirring occasionally, for 5 to 7 minutes more, or until the liquid has evaporated and the mushrooms are firm. Stir in the garlic and minced sage.

*A small farm in Valle d'Aosta*

Preheat the oven to 450°F.

Sprinkle the dough with half of the fontina and top it with the mushroom mixture and the prosciutto. Add the remaining fontina, spreading it in an even layer over the top, and sprinkle with the Parmesan. Arrange the sage leaves decora-tively on the surface and drizzle the *pizza* with the remaining 2 tablespoons oil.

Bake the *pizza* in the lower third of the oven for 15 to 20 minutes, or until the cheese is melted and the crust is golden brown. **Serves 4.**

# Focaccia al Rosmarino

## Flatbread with Rosemary

*Focaccia*, one of Italy's great rustic flatbreads, derives its name from the Latin "focus," meaning hearth, for it was under the ashes in the hearth that it was originally baked. Sometimes depressions are made in *focaccia* in order to trap a variety of wonderful toppings ~ cheese, sea salt or, in this case, rosemary and fruity olive oil.

*1 package (2½ teaspoons) active*
*dry yeast*
*1 cup warm water (108°-110°F.)*
*4 tablespoons extra-virgin olive oil*
*1 teaspoon table salt*

*2¾-3 cups unbleached flour*
*1 tablespoon minced fresh rosemary*
*leaves*
*Coarse sea salt or kosher salt*
*Fresh rosemary sprigs for garnish*

In a bowl, proof the yeast with ¼ cup of the water for 5 minutes, or until foamy. In another bowl, combine the remaining water with 3 tablespoons of the olive oil and the table salt.

In a food processor, combine 2¾ cups of the flour and half the rosemary leaves. With the motor running, add the olive oil mixture and the proofed yeast in a stream through the feed tube, and process for 20 seconds, or until combined well. Gradually add portions of the remaining ¼ cup flour, until the mixture forms a ball. Knead the dough by processing it for 20 seconds.

Put the dough in an oiled bowl and turn it to coat it with the oil. Cover the dough with plastic wrap and a towel and let rise in a warm place for 45 minutes, or until doubled in bulk.

Preheat the oven to 450°F.

On a floured surface, punch down the

dough and roll it into a ¼-inch-thick round. Transfer the round to an oiled heavy baking sheet or a *pizza* pan, and brush it with the remaining oil. Using your fingertips, make impressions in the dough about 1 inch apart. Let the dough rise for 20 minutes. Sprinkle the dough with the remaining rosemary leaves and the coarse salt.

Bake the *focaccia* in the lower third of the oven for 20 minutes, or until it is golden brown. Garnish with the rosemary sprigs. **Makes 1 *focaccia*.**

# Focaccia al Salvio e Cipolle

## Flatbread with Sage and Onions

Here is another example of *focaccia*. Note that the sage appears in both the dough and the topping to render the most resonant results. Serve with a simple green salad and a soup to start, perhaps *Cappelletti in Brodo* (p. 21), and you have the components of a light, but very complete, lunch.

1 package (2½ teaspoons) active dry yeast

1 cup warm water (108°-110°F.)

5 tablespoons olive oil

1½ teaspoons salt

2¾-3 cups unbleached flour

1 tablespoon minced fresh sage leaves or 1½ teaspoons dried

1 onion, thinly sliced

In a bowl, proof the yeast with ¼ cup of the warm water for 5 minutes, or until foamy. In another bowl, combine the remaining water with 3 tablespoons of the olive oil and the table salt.

In a food processor, combine 2¾ cups of the flour and half the sage leaves. With the motor running, add the olive oil mixture and the proofed yeast in a stream through the feed tube, and process for 20 seconds, or until combined well. Gradually add portions of the remaining ¼ cup flour, until the mixture forms a ball. Knead the dough by processing it for 20 seconds.

Put the dough in an oiled bowl and turn it to coat it with oil. Cover the dough with plastic wrap and a towel, and let rise in a warm place for 45 minutes, or until doubled in bulk.

While the dough is rising, in a skillet

*A valley in Tuscany*

over medium heat, cook the onion in 1 tablespoon of the remaining olive oil, stirring occasionally, for 5 minutes.

Preheat the oven to 450°F.

On a floured surface, punch down the dough and roll it into a ¼-inch-thick round. Transfer the round to an oiled heavy baking sheet or a *pizza* pan, and brush it with the remaining oil. Using your fingertips, make impressions in the dough about 1 inch apart. Let the dough rise for 20 minutes. Spread the cooked onions and the remaining sage over the dough.

Bake the *focaccia* in the lower third of the oven for 20 minutes, or until it is golden brown. **Makes 1 *focaccia*.**

# Frutta al Grappa

### Poached Fruit in Grappa

When the luscious fresh fruits of the season have passed, serve this combination of poached pears, raisins, and dried apricots. After the fruits are poached, the liquid in which they were cooked is reduced to a syrup, flavored with *grappa* (the unaged Italian brandy), and poured over the fruit.

*2 Anjou pears*

*Lemon juice*

*2 cups water*

*½ cup sugar*

*1 cinnamon stick, cracked*

*4 whole cloves*

*2 julienne strips lemon zest*

*⅔ cup dried apricots*

*1 cup raisins*

*4 to 6 tablespoons grappa, or to taste*

Peel, quarter, and core the pears, then sprinkle them with the lemon juice.

In a saucepan or shallow skillet, combine the water, sugar, cinnamon stick, cloves, and lemon zest. Bring the mixture to a boil, then reduce the heat and simmer the syrup, stirring occasionally, for 5 minutes, or until it is clear. Add the pears, cover with a round of wax paper, and cook at a bare simmer, turning from time to time, for 5 minutes. Add the apricots and raisins and simmer the fruit, covered, for 10 minutes more, or until the pears are just tender.

Using a slotted spoon, transfer the fruit to a serving dish. Strain the poaching broth into a small saucepan and reduce it to 1 cup over high heat. Stir in the *grappa*. Pour the syrup over the fruit and let it cool. Serve warm or chilled. **Serves 6.**

# Tiramisù

## Coffee and Mascarpone Cream

*Tiramisù*, which means "pick me up" in Italian, is a child in the family of Italian desserts; it was created less than thirty years ago by a chef in Treviso in the Veneto region of Italy. The key ingredients in this dessert are *mascarpone*, an Italian cream cheese, and *biscotti di savoiardi*, both of which can be found at Italian specialty markets.

⅔ cup sugar

¼ cup water

4 large egg yolks

½ teaspoon vanilla

9 ounces mascarpone

4 to 6 tablespoons dark rum, or
    to taste

1 cup heavy cream

12 (about 6 ounces) biscotti di
    savoiardi (Italian ladyfingers)

⅓ cup espresso coffee

3 ounces dark sweet chocolate, grated

In a small saucepan, combine the sugar and water and bring to a boil, stirring, over medium heat. Continue to boil, brushing down the sides of the pan with a brush dipped in cold water, until it reaches the soft-ball stage, or a candy thermometer registers 240°F.

In a bowl, using an electric mixer, beat the yolks until they are combined, then add the sugar syrup in a stream. Beat until cool. Beat in the vanilla.

In a bowl, whisk the *mascarpone* and rum until smooth. In another bowl, beat the heavy cream until it holds soft peaks.

Combine the egg mixture with the *mascar-pone*. Fold in the heavy cream.

Line a 6-cup serving dish with the *bis-cotti* and drizzle the espresso over them. Spoon in the *mascarpone* mixture, smooth-ing the top, and chill, covered with plastic wrap, for at least 3 hours or overnight. Before serving, sprinkle the top with the grated chocolate. **Serves 6.**

# Biscotti alla Nocciola

## Hazelnut Biscotti

At one time the word *biscotti* identified cookies that had been
twice-baked; today, it generally includes all Italian cookies.
This hazelnut rusk ~ which can be dipped in chocolate,
if desired ~ is a classic. Such *biscotti* are traditionally served
with *vin santo*, a dessert wine produced
mainly in Tuscany and Trentino.

*9 tablespoons butter, softened*

*1 egg*

*1 teaspoon vanilla*

*2 cups flour*

*1 cup ground hazelnuts*

*⅔ cup sugar*

*½ teaspoon baking powder*

*Egg glaze, made by*

*beating 1 egg with*

*1 teaspoon water*

In a bowl, using an electric mixer, cream the butter. Add the egg and vanilla and beat until combined well. In another bowl, combine the flour, hazelnuts, sugar, and baking powder. Add the hazelnut mixture to the butter, a little at a time, until the mixture is incorporated. Divide the dough in half and form each half into a 3- by 8-inch rectangle. The dough should be rounded at the sides, slightly higher in the center and tapering off towards the ends. Wrap the dough in plastic wrap and chill for 1 hour.

Preheat the oven to 350°F.

Arrange the rectangles of dough on a buttered baking sheet, brush them with the egg glaze, and score the top of each at ¾-inch intervals. Bake for 1 hour, or until the rectangles are golden brown and dry. (Should they brown too quickly, cover each with

*The park at Villa Borghese, Rome*

foil.) Let the rectangles cool on wire racks for 5 minutes. Cut into ¾-inch slices and allow to cool completely. Store in airtight containers. **Makes about 12 cookies.**

## BISCOTTI CON CIOCCOLATA ALLA NOCCIOLA

**Chocolate-Covered Hazelnut Biscotti**

*1 recipe Hazelnut Biscotti*
*6 ounces dark sweet chocolate,*
*cut into bits*
*4 tablespoons butter*

Set out several cooling racks on the counter. In the top of a double boiler, over hot but not simmering water, melt the chocolate with the butter, stirring. Transfer the melted chocolate to a bowl. Dip each cookie halfway into the chocolate, letting the excess drip back into the bowl. Let the cookies dry on the cooling racks and store in airtight containers. **Makes about 12 cookies.**

# Granita all'Arancia

## Orange Granita

Unlike the smooth texture of the French ices, or sorbets, Italian ices are meant to be grainy ~ coarse, in fact. Tiny crystals of ice should melt on your tongue. There is nothing more cooling on a hot summer day, and *granite* made with citrus fruits are particularly refreshing.

*Grated zest from 1 orange*

*Grated zest from 1 lemon*

*1 cup water*

*½ cup sugar*

*2 cups strained fresh orange juice*

*¼ cup strained fresh lemon juice*

*White & red currants or other*

*fruit for garnish*

In an enameled saucepan over medium heat, combine the zests with the water and sugar, and bring the liquid to a boil. Simmer, stirring occasionally, for 3 minutes, or until the sugar is completely dissolved. Add both fresh juices to the syrup and stir to combine well. Pour the syrup into ice trays or a shallow metal pan and transfer to the freezer. After 1 hour, stir the *granita* to mix the ice crystals into the liquid. Freeze for about 3 hours more, stirring the *granita* every half hour, until its consistency is flaky and grainy, but thoroughly iced. Put scoops of the *granita* in serving dishes and garnish with some of the currants. **Serves 6.**

### *GRANITA ALLE FRAGOLE*
## Strawberry Granita

*1 cup sugar*

*1 cup water*

*1 pound fresh strawberries*

*2 tablespoons lemon juice*

*Fresh berries and mint*

*leaves for garnish*

In a saucepan over medium heat, combine the sugar and water and stir for 2 to 3 minutes, or until the sugar dissolves and the syrup is clear. Let the syrup cool. In a food processor, combine the syrup with the berries and purée. Strain the purée through a fine sieve into a bowl and stir in the lemon juice. Pour the strawberry mixture into ice trays and freeze as directed for Orange Granita. **Serves 6.**

## WEIGHTS

| Ounces and Pounds | Metrics |
|---|---|
| ¼ ounce | 7 grams |
| ⅓ ounce | 10 grams |
| ½ ounce | 14 grams |
| 1 ounce | 28 grams |
| 1¾ ounces | 50 grams |
| 2 ounces | 57 grams |
| 2⅔ ounces | 75 grams |
| 3 ounces | 85 grams |
| 3½ ounces | 100 grams |
| 4 ounces (¼ pound) | 114 grams |
| 6 ounces | 170 grams |
| 8 ounces (½ pound) | 227 grams |
| 9 ounces | 250 grams |
| 16 ounces (1 pound) | 464 grams |
| 1.1 pounds | 500 grams |
| 2.2 pounds | 1,000 grams (1 kilogram) |

## TEMPERATURES

| °F (Fahrenheit) | °C (Centigrade or Celsius) |
|---|---|
| 32 (water freezes) | 0 |
| 108-110 (warm) | 42-43 |
| 140 | 60 |
| 203 (water simmers) | 95 |
| 212 (water boils) | 100 |
| 225 (very slow oven) | 107.2 |
| 245 | 120 |
| 266 | 130 |
| 300 (slow oven) | 149 |
| 350 (moderate oven) | 177 |
| 375 | 191 |
| 400 (hot oven) | 205 |
| 450 | 232 |
| 500 (very hot oven) | 260 |

## LIQUID MEASURES

tsp.: teaspoon
Tbs.: tablespoon

| Spoons and Cups | Metric Equivalents |
|---|---|
| 1 tsp. | 5 milliliters (5 grams) |
| 2 tsp. | 10 milliliters (10 grams) |
| 3 tsp. (1 Tbs.) | 15 milliliters (15 grams) |
| 3⅓ Tbs. | ½ deciliter (50 milliliters) |
| ¼ cup | 59 milliliters |
| ⅓ cup | 1 deciliter less 1⅓ Tbs. |

| Spoons and Cups | Metric Equivalents |
|---|---|
| ⅓ cup + 1 Tbs. | 1 deciliter (100 milliliters) |
| 1 cup | ¼ liter less 1¼ Tbs. |
| 1 cup + 1¼ Tbs. | ¼ liter |
| 2 cups | ½ liter less 2½ Tbs. |
| 2 cups + 2½ Tbs. | ½ liter |
| 4 cups | 1 liter less 1 deciliter |
| 4⅓ cups | 1 liter (1,000 milliliters) |

# INDEX

## Picture Credits

Picture Perfect: 1; 48; 61; 63; 81; 85; 91.

Boys Syndication/Michael Boys: 2-3;14-15. Richard Felber: 11;
47; 89. Jerry Simpson: 12; 25; 33. Margaret Courtney-Clark:
7; 17; 23; 51. Alan Richardson: 18; 39; 45; 65; 74; 86.

John Heseltine: 20. John Sims: 27; 72. Anthony Blake/Picture
Perfect: 29; 78. ADNA/Mondadori Press: 36; 53; 55; 57; 67.

Ellen Silverman: 40; 58; 68; 93. Elizabeth Watt: 83.

Vadim Sokolov/Picture Perfect: 96.